I Am a Good Citizen

By Mary Ann Hoffman

Gareth Stevens
Publishing

Please visit our Web site, www.garethstevens.com. For a free color catalog of all our high-quality books, call toll free 1-800-542-2595 or fax 1-877-542-2596.

Library of Congress Cataloging-in-Publication Data

Hoffman, Mary Ann.
 I am a good citizen / Mary Ann Hoffman.
   p. cm. — (Kids of character)
 Includes index.
 ISBN 978-1-4339-4851-0 (pbk.)
 ISBN 978-1-4339-4852-7 (6-pack)
 ISBN 978-1-4339-4850-3 (library binding)
 1. Citizenship–United States–Juvenile literature. I. Title.
 JK1759.H64 2011
 323.60973–dc22
                                    2010034633

First Edition

Published in 2011 by
Gareth Stevens Publishing
111 East 14th Street, Suite 349
New York, NY 10003

Editor: Mary Ann Hoffman
Designer: Christopher Logan

Photo credits: Cover, pp. 1, 7, 11, 13, 15, 17, 19 Shutterstock.com; p. 5 Jupiter Images/Comstock/Thinkstock; p. 9 RL Productions/Digital Vision/Thinkstock; pp. 21 iStockphoto.com.

Printed in the United States of America

CPSIA compliance information: Batch #CW11GS: For further information contact Gareth Stevens, New York, New York at 1-800-542-2595.

Table of Contents

Boldface words appear in the glossary.

What Is a Good Citizen?

Good **citizens** care about themselves and their community. Good citizens are helpful. They treat others fairly. Good citizens **obey** rules. They take care of their things and the things that belong to others.

In the Neighborhood

Therese likes to play and have fun. She likes for other children to play and have fun, too. Therese shares her toys. Therese is a good citizen.

James helps keep his neighborhood clean. He **recycles** used papers, bottles, and cans. He does not **litter**. James is a good citizen.

Alice and Max obey **traffic** rules. They look at the traffic light to know when they can cross the street. They look both ways before they step into the street. Alice and Max are good citizens.

At School

Beth helps at school. She helps friends who cannot do things for themselves. She picks up books, crayons, and pencils that have fallen on the floor. She helps her friends read. Beth is a good citizen.

Tom plays on the school team. He waits his turn. He is happy when other players on the team do well. Tom has good **manners** even when his team loses. Tom is a good citizen.

Lee pays attention in school. She listens when others are speaking. She does her own work. She finishes her work on time. She helps in the classroom. Lee is a good citizen.

Sara is running for class president. She wants to do good things for her classmates. Sara is a good citizen.

At Home

Joe helps keep his yard and sidewalk clean. He puts his toys away. He picks up papers and sticks from the grass. He sweeps the sidewalk. He rakes the leaves. Joe is a good citizen.

Glossary

citizen: someone who lives in a place

litter: to throw trash onto the ground

manners: being thoughtful of others

obey: to listen to and follow directions

recycle: to use again

traffic: cars, trucks, and other moving objects on a street

For More Information

Books

Serrano, John. *Being a Good Citizen*. Pelham, NY: Newmark Learning, 2010.

Small, Mary. *Being a Good Citizen: A Book About Citizenship*. Minneapolis, MN: Picture Window Books, 2006.

Web Sites

Citizenship
www.timeforcitizenship.org/citizenship.php
Read about why we need good citizens. Learn what you can do to become a good citizen.

Kids Next Door
www.hud.gov/kids
Play games and learn how you can be a good citizen.

Index